I0080911

Above

ALL ELSE!

ERIKA CLAYTON

Copyright Notice

Above All Else

by Erika Clayton

© 2023, Erika Clayton
erika_tolbert@yahoo.com

Published by Anointed Fire House

www.anointedfirehouse.com

Cover Design by Anointed Fire House

ISBN-13: 978-1-955557-43-6

This book contains material protected under International and Federal Copyright Laws and Treaties. Any unauthorized reprint or use of this material is prohibited. No part of this book may be reproduced or transmitted in any form or by any means, electronic or mechanical, including photocopying, recording, or by any information storage and retrieval system without express written permission from the author/publisher.

I have tried to recreate events, locations, and conversations from my memories of them. In order to maintain their anonymity in some instances, I have changed the names of individuals and places and I may have changed some identifying characteristics and details such as physical properties, occupations and places of residence.

Although the author and publisher have made every effort to ensure that the information in this book was correct at press time, the author and publisher do not assume and hereby disclaim any liability to any party for any loss, damage, or disruption caused by errors or omissions, whether such errors or omissions result from negligence, accident, or any other cause.

"Above all else, guard your heart for everything you do flows from it. Keep your mouth free of perversity; Keep corrupt talk far from your lips. Let your eyes look straight ahead; fix your gaze directly before you. Give careful thoughts to the paths for your feet and be steadfast in all your ways. Do not turn to the right or left, keep your foot from evil."

-Proverbs 4:23-27

To my Sweetheart, my love, my husband, John:

- Thank you for your loving leadership and support. I am blessed to be your wife. I love you infinity and beyond.

To my baby girls, Grace and Faith:

- Your names alone exemplify God's love towards you. I pray that you both will always be who He's created you to be. May you always love the Lord with all of your heart, mind and soul. Mommy loves you always to infinity and beyond.

To my family and friends:

- Thank you all for being in my life and allowing me to be in yours. May God's goodness and mercy follow you all the days of your life.

Table of Contents

Introduction

My prayer for you is that as you read this book, you will be overwhelmed with encouragement, edification, wisdom, and strength. Most importantly, I pray that you are filled with God's truth, no matter where you currently are in life. The love that God has for you and I is unconditional and promising, regardless of whether you are a firm believer or just a curious reader. I want you to know that repentance is near to all who ask God for it. It is not God's will that anyone should perish without the truth of redemption through His Son, Jesus Christ.

Grace and mercy are God's incredible gifts to us all, and so is the gift of repentance. God's love language to us is grace and mercy or, better yet, gracious and merciful. God gives us His love, not necessarily because we deserve it or have done anything to earn it; God graciously gives us His unconditional love so that we may acknowledge our sins and desire an intimate relationship with Him above all else! This is so that our hearts are healthy, both physically and spiritually.

Heart

Why are our hearts important? Our hearts are important because they pump blood throughout our bodies, delivering oxygen and nutrients to our cells and removing waste products. For the most part, we are all aware that the heart is a particularly important organ in our bodies. So, on the physical side of it, we are often told that in order to maintain a healthy heart, we are to eat healthier foods, get proper exercise, regularly check and maintain a proper blood pressure level and, of course, give up any bad habits that could potentially induce or lead to heart disease. However, the physical aspects of the heart are not the only ways to induce heart disease. If we are not consciously guarding our hearts in a healthy way, we will miss the "Above All Else" approach to life. The fruit of our familial relationships, intimate relationships, friendships, professional relationships, and so on stems from our hearts' spiritual posture. As I was reading about and researching the physical matter that God created to protect of hearts, such as our rib cages, Proverbs 4:23 seem to come to life. It reads, "Guard your heart for everything you do flows from it." This scripture alone brought forth so much understanding regarding the concept of the rib cage. The human rib cage is said and known to be one of the body's best defenses against injury from impact. It is known to be flexible, yet strong. If our hearts are being physically guarded and protected by our rib cages, then how much more should we positively guard them spiritually?!

Lord, we say we love you with our mouths, but our hearts, flesh, and actions say otherwise. Lord, we say we trust you, but we find ourselves putting more trust into this world than we put in you. Our careers, our degrees, our families, our friends, green paper (money); all of these earthly things tend to come and go. We begin to idolize our success within this world, intentionally or unintentionally.

"No one can serve two masters, for you will hate one and love the other; you will be devoted to one and despise the other. You cannot serve God and be enslaved to money." - Matthew 6:24

3

How is it that we often seek guidance, love, wisdom, confidence, protection, happiness, comfort, and confirmation from within the world, rather than seeking God for everything?! We tend to fight our spiritual battles with the temporary weapons of the world. We do this assuming that those carnal weapons would fill the emptiness within us. Because of our sinful, fallen nature, we are often inclined to do whatever pleases our flesh. I know exactly what it is like to run from God and ignore the signs and promptings of His Spirit! Those unctions constantly tugged on my heart. We begin to shut God out and wander away from God's loving guidance. We often get lost within our struggles. We then try to handle our situations and circumstances on our own, only to fail trying to fix what only God can mend within us and within our lives. The definition of mend is to repair something that is broken or damaged. Only God can mend your heart and spirit. No matter the situation or circumstances, God, our Creator, is equipped with everything He needs to re-polish our hearts and make us whole again within Him.

During one of my quiet moments with God, I believe He spoke to my anxious heart. He said, "Longevity and joy are greater than temporary happiness! Erika, build your foundation on the joy of the Lord, for happiness fades away and loses its desire throughout seasons." Oddly enough, it reminded me of Ecclesiastes 3:3, which reads, "For everything there is a season, a time for every activity under heaven. A time to be born and a time to die. A time to plant and a time to harvest. A time to kill and a time to heal. A time to tear down and a time to build up. A time to cry and a time to laugh. A time to grieve and a time to dance. A time to scatter stones and a time to gather stones. A time to embrace and a time to turn away. A time to search and a time to quit searching. A time to keep and a time to throw away. A time to tear and a time to mend. A time to be quiet and a time to speak. A time to love and a time to hate. A time for war and a time for peace." Reading this scripture assures me that happiness is sure to fade away! However, there is a joy that only God can provide; this is a joy that the world is unable to take. A joy that continues to sing songs of praise and gratitude from our hearts to God despite our circumstances. It is only in our weakness that God's power is made strong. God's still small voice reminds us to keep going so that our fights are not about us! God knew us before we were formed in our mothers' wombs! This means He knows our hardships, our struggles, our doubts, our failures, our goals, and our desires, even the ones that are not His. Yet, that is! God still loves us and works on us until our desires become His desires; that is, until our hearts reflect His characteristics. He has a plan and a purpose for each of our lives.

Growing up in a one-parent household with my earthly dad not always one hundred percent present, I must admit that his absence affected the way I went about life to some degree, both for the good and for the worst. Every summer, my siblings and I would travel to Alabama to visit my grandparents and spend time with them;

that is good ole hot, country Alabama. As I reflect on those warm, humid summers, not only was it a summer vacation, but a place of peace and joy to be surrounded by God's beautiful nature. As a child, I have always believed there is a God. My grandmother taught me how to pray. Every night before bed, there was a prayer I would utter that I have never forgotten to date. If you've been blessed to have a loving, praying grandmother, you've likely heard this prayer before as well. "Now, I lay me down to sleep. I pray the Lord my soul to keep. If I should die before I wake, I pray the Lord my soul to take." Although this simple prayer may seem small, it allowed my grandmother to plant a seed of prayer in my heart. Even as a young child, I was aware of God. However, my perspective and experience with my earthly father whom I could physically see made it exceedingly difficult for me to trust my Heavenly Father whom I cannot physically see. The dad I could see didn't protect me from the molestation of my stepdad by simply being present and providing a covering and a sense of identity. How could my Heavenly Father whom I can't physically see truly love and protect me? How could my Heavenly Father allow me to experience such a traumatic encounter? How could I trust God? It led me to unconsciously run from God and ignore the root issue (the sin of mankind, that is). It was not that my dad did not love me, and it certainly wasn't that God didn't love me, after all, God adored me then as much as He does now. However, my sinful nature and brokenness led me to believe otherwise.

The seeds of molestation that were planted in my childhood produced the fruit of promiscuity in my teenage years, causing me to go from one relationship to another. How in the world did I ever assume or think that getting into another relationship right after ending one would be healthy? Like me, if you haven't been saved your entire life, you may understand the sinful thought-pattern associated with that decision. Dysfunction breeds unwise behavior and decisions. There was a seed of trauma deposited in me that made it easy for me to quickly end a relationship and immediately enter into another one. I was surly a no-tolerance young girl when it came to relationships. If I saw any sign of disrespect, the relationship was over. Even in my ignorance of sin, I had a glimpse of my worth but not the full picture. The no tolerance for disrespect that I had then wasn't because I was tough or that I had a strong heart. It was the fruit of my brokenness. I guarded my heart out of fear. I attempted to end any relationship I deemed to be toxic before anymore damage could be done to my heart; this way, my process of moving on wouldn't be as painful—or so I thought. So, I ended up in relationships with men I would not have given an ounce of attention to if I'd run into the arms of my Creator (God) instead of the arms of another broken, sinful human. Can you think of a moment or season where you thought you were on your own, but as you look back, all you see is God's amazing grace?! Oh, what a joy it is to know God was with you all along! And if you currently find yourself in that moment or season feeling as if you're alone, let me remind you now that no matter how broken, lost, or confused you may be, God loves you more than you could ever know!

Extended Grace

"Amazing grace how sweet the sound that saved a wretch like me! I once was lost, but now I am found; was blind but now I see'.' This is a very catchy tune, and I am sure you have heard it before. I remember having an epiphany pertaining to that song. Granted, I had heard it before, but it did not mean anything until I utterly understood the depth of the words of that song. Until I understood how God's amazing grace was and continues to cover me every day of my life, and how He chose me long before I chose Him. Without God's Word and before Christ, we could not see our sinful dysfunction because we live in such a broken world. Consequently, our sin became comfortable. I know what you are thinking. "God knows my heart" ... I cannot count or remember the many times I thought or said those words while partaking in my sin. I uttered those words in my attempt to avoid the harsh feeling of condemnation. It is true that God knows our hearts, after all, God is omniscient. He knows everything. How many times do we try to rationalize our sins with those exact words? It was safe to say that God knew my heart, but oh how I was missing out on the beauty of His heart. I can vividly remember being in bondage to my sin. I was drinking, smoking, and sleeping with my "boyfriend"—a man who was not my husband. Those words sprang from my heart like a song, and while those words are definitely true, He loved us long before we ever loved Him! I had a fleshly sense of entitlement, as if God owed me something because I was His child and He created me. Boy, was I wrong! Why is it that we try to hold onto a fleshly sense of entitlement to God's blessings in all of our sinfulness? The blessings that God showers upon us in our sinfulness are nothing short of His unmerited grace towards us. He uses His grace to draw us to Himself. Romans 3:23 reads, "For all have sinned; and fall short of the glory of God. And are justified by his grace as a gift, through the redemption that is in Christ Jesus." It is His love that draws us to repentance.

My former pastor asked a question to the congregation during one of his sermons. The question that was proposed brought a healthy conviction to my heart; this question resonated with me and brought

15

forth understanding. The question asked was, "Do you love Him, or do you just need Him?" I answered to myself, "I mean yeah; I love and need God!" After pondering on that question, I truly had to examine my heart. Have my prayers been selfish? Have I been seeking God to fix my life and clean up the mess I made? Do I simply want Him to make me happy? Granted, seeking God for restoration, guidance, and help was not the problem. He wants joy for all His children. He wants His children to fully depend on Him. However, expecting God to honor my requests without me having to lay down my old life and strengthen my relationship with Him led me to question the sincerity of my love for Him. The sex, partying, drinking, smoking, and living in my intentional sin—I was trying to justify my ways while singing the same ole song, "God knows my heart." I repeatedly told myself, "I am young... I love God," and yet, I was choosing my own ways over His. My mindset was of the world. I thought to myself, "You only get one life!" And while this is true, why not live it the way God intended for us to live it?

The Bible says that Jesus heals in accordance with our faith. There was a woman who suffered for twelve years with constant bleeding. This woman had faith that if she could only touch the hem of Jesus' robe, she would be healed (see Matthew 9:19). Jesus said to her, "Daughter be encouraged. Your faith has made you well!" How amazing is that?! How many of us have needed to desperately touch the hem of Jesus' robe for healing? I certainly have, especially after years of combating internal brokenness, insecurities, rejection, fear, anxieties, and inadequacies. Desperately finding my way into God's presence brought about healing from within. I felt as if Jesus spoke those exact words to my heart. "Daughter, be encouraged. Your faith has made you well." There are numerous stories of miraculous faith within the Bible that I encourage you to read; they will bring forth restoration and healing.

"From Heaven the Lord looks down and sees all mankind; from his dwelling place he watches all who live on earth- He who forms the hearts of all, who considers everything they do. No King is saved by the size of his army, no warrior escapes by his great strength. A horse is a vain hope for deliverance; despite all it's great strength it cannot save, but the eyes of the Lord are on those who fear him, on those whose hope is in his unfailing love, to deliver them from death and keep them alive in famine. We wait in hope for the Lord; he is our shield, in him our hearts rejoice, for we trust in his holy name. May your unfailing love be with us, Lord even as we put our hope in you."

---Psalm 33:13-22 (NIV)

The Blessing of a Closed Door

How could a closed door be a blessing, especially if what's behind it is something you want? I know that during those rough seasons of our lives, we all must endure. We all have made the mistake of questioning and trying to understand why the door was closed when God knew we desired to have it open. It becomes hard for us, as humans, to wrap our heads around the concept of a closed door being a blessing. However, that shut door just may be one of the many blessings we receive from God. Proverbs 20:24 says, "The Lord directs our steps, so why try to understand everything along the way?" Many times, when things seemed to not go my way or the way that I expected it to go, it was simply because I had gone ahead of God; I had not prayed for direction or waited for His response. The flesh will cause you to become anxious, impatient, weary, and doubtful. This is typically how failure roots itself because our eyes are not fixed on our Creator; instead, we seem to fixate on our circumstances. God usually keeps us going at a steady pace for a specific reason. He is such a good Father and Teacher that He wants us to learn and not miss out on the lessons He is trying to teach us in any given season.

I know it is exceedingly difficult to mentally process how a closed door could be a blessing, especially when we see the door shutting. How did this happen? I wanted to hold tightly to that relationship, even though it was not good for me. I wanted to stay at that job because I was comfortable. I wanted to get that degree. I wanted to start the business. I wanted to....I..I..I. Eventually, God will allow you to see how selfish your desires may truly be. Granted, the intentions of our desires may not be bad at all. In fact, some of them may come from God. However, when our desires aren't within His will for us, He often shows us how we've never fully consulted Him about our plans. This is largely because in our human fragility, we tend to assume that we're the author of our lives, and somehow, we're in control. "We can make many plans, but the Lord's purpose will prevail" (Proverbs 19:21). I just find it super amazing that God's plans are always better than the plans we've chosen for ourselves. Although God gives everyone free will, if our hearts are open to His will, He will certainly change our plans. Be prepared to have some things shaken up in your life. Be prepared for some plucking, pruning, planting, discomfort, and growth.

I remember giving my ex-fiancé an ultimatum around the second or third year of our relationship. I told him that he had five years to figure out if he was going to make me his wife or not. I told him that by year five, if the decision had not been made, I would leave the relationship. See, I've always had the desire to do things the right way, but the problem came when I decided to make it happen on my own, with my own demands. I did not realize that God's hand was on my life, and that He was calling me to Himself. I spent 5 ½ years in that relationship being disobedient to God in my ignorance. Did I know that I was being disobedient? Of course not! However, ignorance didn't give me a pass for my error. The seeds of my sins produced the fruit of my consequences, but God was merciful. The day he proposed (in public, to be exact) in the presence of both our families set the stage of constant pressure. Not to mention, we were celebrating our five-year mark of being together. There I was, in the midst of being ignorant regarding my worth in Christ. I stood there filled with temporary happiness, completely ignoring the lack of peace I felt in that moment. I was broken, flawed, insecure, confused, and oh so prideful. Our empty voids fed one another's. When I said yes, I completely ignored the fact that I had no peace within. I rationalized and had this pseudo belief that my plans were coming to fruition. "My plans" and not "God's plans." Oh, how naïve of me! I found myself becoming extremely miserable, trying to plan a wedding. I remember the night God proved Himself to me. It was the night I found myself on my bathroom floor crying and pouring out my heart to Him all night. Even in my disobedience and ignorance, God heard my sincere cry for Him to rescue me from it all. As I continued to seek after God, and as He was purging my heart and renewing my mind, the man that had proposed months prior and proclaimed his love for me told me that he wasn't "in love" with me anymore. He absolutely had no idea that the feeling was mutual. He did not know the prayer I'd desperately prayed to God was about me getting out of that relationship. I truly believe that in that moment of me having a contrite heart and earnestly praying to God,

He began to shift some things in the spiritual realm. He began stripping strongholds, soul ties, and demons that once connected me to that relationship away from me. The closer I drew to God, the more my ex and I grew apart. When I gave up trying to have my way and allowed God to orchestrate His plans in my life, I recovered my peace. Jesus took over my heart in such a way that I knew it was no one but Him. Not me, not my ex, but God! Jesus is the Rock you never want to exchange for a diamond.

The seasons of trials and faith are only growth storms. The pruning and molding process God takes us through could seem painful in the moment, however, in the end, it is so beautiful and rewarding. He gently strips away our comfort and the things we're so accustomed to because they hinder our growth. He does this so that He can place us where He needs us to be. Healthy elevation requires separation and reconciliation. Separation from our own lustful desires and reconciliation to God's will.

Flow of Growth

The way God created us is so unique.
As I was reading information on the blood
flow of our hearts, I found the information
to be quite astounding. God is truly the
greatest Creator there is! I read that our
hearts consist of four chambers in which
blood flows. "Blood enters the right atrium
and passes through the right ventricle. The
right ventricle pumps the blood to the lungs
where it becomes oxygenated. The
oxygenated blood is brought back to the
heart by the pulmonary veins which enter
the left atrium" (courtesy of MedlinePlus
from the National Library of Medicine). God
uniquely designed the physical process, so

that our blood could freely flow to our hearts. What stood out to me during my reading was the physical process. Without the blood passing through the proper channels in our hearts, oxygen could not be supplied to the various organs of our bodies. Oxygen is what gives us life. Now, let us investigate the spiritual matter of our hearts' process. We have been redeemed by the blood of Christ that was shed for the redemption of our sins; this is so that we may be reconciled back to God. However, there is a spiritual process that God wants to send our hearts through; this process is similar to the physical process, and it allows the Word of God to supply the oxygen of life that our spirit needs. We must make the choice of allowing the blood of Jesus to pass through each point of our hearts, thus uprooting all toxins such as pride, unforgiveness, bitterness, fear, regret, discontentment, and everything that could hinder the flow of growth that supplies the oxygen of life. The oxygen of life includes joy, peace, contentment, and wholeness.

There will be storms that God will lead you into that no one or nothing in this world can get you out of but Him alone! He leads us into such storms so that we may run to Him. This allows Him to move, thus provoking us to BELIEVE Him. It reminds me of how Jesus told the disciples to meet Him on the other side of the lake. He led the disciples into a preordained storm, not to frighten them but to build their trust in Him. Why is it when a storm comes or our lives seem to be completely spiraling out of control that we instantly assume the enemy (the devil himself) is behind our rough pastures? Oddly enough, Satan may be the culprit behind our storms in some situations. Even so, it just may be God trying to get our attention. This is especially true if He only hears from us when we are in the midst of our storms. Remember, God is a jealous God. He wants to be the only one on the throne of our hearts.

When I was experiencing a broken engagement back in 2017, my human mind could not wrap itself around the concept of yet another failed relationship, even though there had been no trace of peace left in that relationship. As I look back, I realize that I was in a storm of decisions. Do I hang onto or release my will, or do I embrace God's will for me? A will that seemed so far-fetched and foreign to my understanding. However, when you bump your head long enough, you become susceptible to God's wisdom. Oh, how grateful I am to have surrendered to the leading of the Holy Spirit in that moment by making a choice then that would still be affecting me right now. I now have an amazing husband and twin baby girls. Waiting on God, by far, isn't always easy, but it certainly is always worth it.

In today's generation, people idolize God's blessings, along with things and deities that are not of Him. It is very evident that many worship God for what is in His hand, not what's in His heart. Many times, we want to tag scripture to our disobedience, but this hinders us more than it helps us. As I walk with Christ through this life of mine, I am still growing in ways I could not have imagined, and not because of anything that I have done or am doing, but because of God's infinite love, grace, mercy, and wisdom. It is truly such a humbling experience to choose and walk with God. I mean—yes, I was certainly in the "God knows my heart" bunch. I was continually and intentionally living my life of sin, expecting God to just help me in my time of need. After this, I thought I'd just go back to living as I pleased. Granted, we are NOT our sin! God hates sin, but He LOVES us!

When Christ enters your heart, you become a new creation. "So, from now on we regard no one from a worldly point of view. Though we once regarded Christ in this way, we do so no longer. Therefore, if anyone is in Christ, the new creation has come the old has gone, the new is here" (2 Corinthians

5:17). You do not walk the same, talk the same, or react the same. You do not allow your flesh to dictate the direction of your feet or your actions. This is the walk we choose once Christ enters our hearts; we make a conscious decision every day to get it right, not out of perfectionism, because we all fall short of God's glory, but out of a heart that's surrendered to God's will.

Acts 20:21 reminds us to "turn to God in repentance and have faith in the Lord Jesus." Once I became aware of my identity in Christ and what I mean to Him, it became hard for me to even attempt to return to my foolish ways. There is too much at risk to go back to what the Lord delivered me from. I cannot return to the sins of my flesh; these include the partying, the drinking, smoking, fornication, pornography, manipulation, and selfishness. It is easy to have faith and trust God when everything is going right, but this is not when our faith is put to the test. Our faith is put to the test when everything seems to be going wrong! Your faith shows up when you lose a job, experience family issues, suffer through the loss of a relationship, when friendships are broken, find yourself buried under financial burdens, or the enemy simply reminds you of your past failures. These can all be overwhelming, so much so that when such difficulties arise, the word "faith" may be the last thing that springs to the forefront of your mind. However, I would like to believe and suggest that it is in those very moments that the strength of our faith is truly exercised. Exercise is good for the heart. It gets the blood pumping and flowing through your body. It increases the heart rate, thus allowing your body to burn all of its unnecessary toxins. It also produces healthy muscles, strength and endurance. In our moments of trials and throughout the many unwanted and unforeseen circumstances that we are presented with, we must understand that any and every measure of resistance is an opportunity for us to use and strengthen our faith-muscle.

I have made many bad decisions that I am not happy about because I am sure those decisions broke God's heart. I have had sex outside of marriage, I have partied in clubs, I have smoked, I have hung with the wrong crowd, and yet, God kept His eyes on me. Nonetheless, I am grateful for my mistakes because they are what drew me closer to God. While God knows our hearts, He also knows what is in them and what we have not laid at His feet. I remember carrying around burdens that my little shoulders were not strong enough to carry. In my attempt to pour out to God in one of my lowest moments, He had me write out the question: "Can I use you?" That question helped me to realize that I was still harboring and holding onto things He needed me to lay at His feet. His Holy Spirit began to minister to my heart as the tears flowed from my eyes. "Can I use you? Things did not go as you planned, but that is okay. My plan is better. Can I use you? You have experienced heartbreak, but throughout it all, you came to realize that I am love! I am trying to use you, but I need you to let go of the bondage of your past; I need you to let go of your fears and your failures because only 'I know the plans and the thoughts that

I have towards you. Plans to prosper you and not to harm you, but to give you a hope and a future'" (Jeremiah 29:11). Get into a covenant with God and watch Him change your name, after all, God has a way of making all things new. God has always been in the name-changing business. In the Bible, God changed Abram's name to Abraham, Sarai to Sarah, Jacob to Israel, Simon to Peter, Saul to Paul—just to name a few. God is surely in the business of changing your name today! Our loving and gracious Heavenly Father not only changes our names, but He establishes new identities for us that are attached to the names He's given us! We are precious in God's sight, and the moment He changes our names is a moment to forever cherish. In Isaiah 43:1, God completely blew my mind! "But now, thus says the Lord, he who created you, O

Jacob, he who formed you, O Israel: Fear not, for I have redeemed you; I have called you by name, you are mine" (Isaiah 43:1). Now, I will like to bring out the revelation that God shared with me as I read that particular verse. As we know, God has always been in the name-changing business. However, in this verse of scripture, God had already changed Jacob's name to Israel, so why did the Lord refer to him as Jacob again? Maybe, because Jacob, in all of his humanity, slightly forgot who God Himself said that he was (Israel)! God said "I created you, O Jacob." The word create means to bring something into existence. God said, "He who formed you, O Israel." The word formed means to bring together/or combine something. God had to remind Jacob that he was now Israel and that he did not have to fear because the Lord had redeemed him and given him a new name and identity. Hence, He said, "I have called you by name; you are mine."

Let's be honest, growing hurts, plainly put! Growth challenges us to renew our minds from all that some of us may have ever known. Growth drags us out of our comfort zones. In my comfort, I am not the on-stage speaking type of individual, but our omnipotent, loving Heavenly Father occasionally calls me to that lane. I've said to the Lord:

- "God, I am not a public speaker!"
- "God, I talk fast when I'm nervous!"
- "God, my hands are sweaty!"

I have uttered every excuse you can imagine. Yet, I end up speaking and He uses me when I get out of His way. To do something you have never done before could always be a bit freighting, intimidating, and overwhelming. Nevertheless, it untimely leaves the right amount of space for God to reveal Himself in a way you have never seen.

Comparison is the thief of all joy! I am sure you have heard this statement before. Quite honestly, it is absolutely true. If we do not know and remind ourselves of how much of a treasure we are to God or how we have our own uniqueness and purposes, we can easily slip into the trap of comparison. We must be careful not to envy and covet the journeys of others. Many of us covet relationships, marriage, children, and careers. Some people covet the personalities of other people, while some covet other people's gifts and purposes. Crazy; right? But, it is true. And the issue stems and starts in the heart, and not from what we see.

Have I been jealous before? Definitely! Have I coveted the idea of relationships or marriage? Certainly! Have I compared my purpose, gifts and faith-walk to the journeys of others? Sigh...yes! However, God showed me those toxic ideologies in my heart that needed to be uprooted; this had to be followed by repentance. Repentance means to intentionally turn away from sin and surrender to God. When you choose to celebrate and support others on their paths, it makes the enemy (Satan himself) mad, because God uproots those toxic seeds, thus disabling the enemy from using them. How many of you have ever worked hard by God's grace to accomplish something that mattered to you, only to have a lack of support and a bit of jealousy thrown your way? In some fashion, shape or form, we all may have experienced this, but DO NOT water those seeds of envy and jealousy in your heart.

Above all else, we are to guard our hearts from envy, jealousy, and covetousness. When we covet and are jealous of the journeys of others, what we are truly telling God in our hearts is that we do not believe that He can do for us what He has done for them. God can do anything but lie! God has anointed us all to stay in the lane He has specifically chosen for us. As I write this, I am reminded of Jesus' words in Mark 7:20, which reads, "It is what comes from the inside that defiles you. For from within, out of a person's heart come evil thoughts, sexual immorality, theft, murder, adultery, greed, wickedness, deceit, lustful desires, envy, slander, pride, and foolishness. All these things come from within; they are what defiles you." Therefore, it is vital to guard the inner purity of our hearts so that the righteousness of God can be produced from the seeds God has sown in our hearts. When we stand before God, we will not just be held accountable for what we said, but we will be held accountable for what's truly in our hearts. Remember, out of the abundance of the heart, the mouth speaks.

"Blessed are the pure in heart, for they shall see God" (Matthew 5:8). Our hearts are often referred to as the center of our being. This includes our minds, will, and emotions (soul). Tending to the spiritual health of our hearts is vital; it allows us to produce God's character and reflect our identities in Him.

Identity Mirror

Who am I? Who are you? What reflects your identity? According to Google.com, the definition of identity is: "the fact of being who or what a person or thing is." Also, according to Google.com, the definition of mirror is: "a reflective surface, now typically of glass coated with a metal amalgam, that reflects a clear image."

Now that we have gotten the definition of these two words out of the way, let's simplify the context of our identities by looking at our biblical identity in Christ.

(Genesis 1:27)

"So God created human beings in his own image. In the image of God he created them; male and female he created them."

(Ephesians 1:4-7)

"Even before he made the world, God loved us and chose us in Christ to be holy and without fault in his eyes. God decided in advance to adopt us into his own family by bringing us to himself through Jesus Christ. This is what he wanted to do, and it gave him great pleasure. So we praise God for the glorious grace he has poured out on us who belong to his dear son. He is so rich in kindness and grace that he purchased our freedom with the blood of his son and forgave our sins."

(John 1:10-13)

"He came into the very world he created, but the world didn't recognize him. He came to his own people, and even they rejected him. But to all who believed in him and accepted him, he gave the right to become children of God. They are reborn – not with a physical birth resulting from human passion or plan, but a birth that comes from God."

(Romans 6:4-10)

"For we died and were buried with Christ by baptism. And just as Christ was raised from the dead by the glorious power of the Father, now we may also live new lives. Since we have been united with him in his death, we will also be raised to life as he was. We know that our old sinful selves were crucified with Christ so that sin might lose its power in our lives. We are no longer slaves to sin. For when we died with Christ we were set free from the power of sin. And since we died with Christ we also know that we will live with him. We are sure of this because Christ was raised from the dead, and he will never die again. Death no longer has any power over him. When he died, he died once to break the power of sin. But now that he lives, he lives for the glory of God. So you also should consider yourselves to be dead to the power of sin and alive to God through Christ Jesus."

(1 Peter 2:9)

"For you are a chosen people. You are royal priests, a holy nation. God's very own possession. As a result, you can show others the goodness of God, for he called you out of darkness into his wonderful light."

(2 Corinthians 5:17)

"Anyone who belongs to Christ has become a new person. The old life is gone; a new life has begun."

If God were to remove everything from the Earth, would you know who you are? God instructs us in His Word to store up our treasures in Heaven. "Do not store up for yourselves treasures on earth, where moths and vermin destroy, and where thieves break in and steal. But store up for yourselves treasures in heaven, where moths and vermin do not destroy, and where thieves do not break in and steal. For where your treasure is, there your heart will be also" (Matthew 6:19-21).

Money, materialistic possessions, positions, titles and things we may deem worthy on this Earth will only produce natural fruit. It will not produce treasures for us to store in Heaven if we are doing it for our names' sake and not God's. Only what we do for Christ will last. All good things come from above. In a world that feeds our insecurities, fears, doubts, and flesh, I want to encourage you, in this moment, to look in the mirror and ask yourself, "Who am I and what defines me?" Is it your career? Is it your relationship status? Is it your bank account? Is it your education? Is it your home? Is it your car? Is it materialistic in nature? If God removed these things from you, would you know who you are? Would you be able to face yourself in the mirror and know who you are and who you belong to? Would you be able to lift your head with the same high spirits and integrity as before? God wants the absolute best for us, but our success should never become our identities in this world. You are more than your failures or your accomplishments here on Earth. Are the treasures of your heart healthy? Who do you belong to?

Now that technology and social media have tremendously grown and continues to grow, they can either cause you to question your identity or stand firm in your identity. Do not allow other people's "social highlights" to cause you to question/challenge your own identity or season. I remember being in that season like it was yesterday. I was unconsciously allowing social media to change my mood, my attitude, and my actions, along with my mind, will, and emotions! I want to encourage you to not give away your peace and joy by being distracted by "social highlights." You are not behind! You are not a failure! You are just distracted by the "social highlights" of others. Everyone has their own journey and everyone experiences the many seasons of this event we call life. Your peace is in the present, not in the future. Be mindful of God's presence in your present moments.

How can we focus on what God has for us if our eyes are on another person's journey? Often, we slow up our own processes and progress by watching other fruit trees grow, instead of watering our own. I love the story of Job in the Bible. Job was a man of complete integrity. He was blameless; he feared God and stayed away from evil. One day, Satan was prowling around, seeking whom he could devour, and

God asked Satan, "Have you noticed my servant, Job?" God had given Satan permission to test Job because He knew Job's faithfulness and integrity towards Him. Satan told God, "You have always put a wall of protection around him and his property. You have made him prosper in everything he does. Reach out and snatch away everything from him, and he will surly curse you." So, the Lord gave Satan permission to test Job; to do whatever he wished, with the exception of causing him physical harm. Throughout all the testing and devastation, including the loss of his family, finances and property, Job remained faithful to God. Job still had the heart of a true worshiper and servant. He said, "I came from my mother's womb naked, and I will be naked when I leave. The Lord gave me what I had and the Lord has taken it away. Praise the name of the Lord!" Job understood that everything he had belonged to God anyhow. He was just stewarding what had been given to him by God, so he was able to praise God even after it had all been taken away from him. The Lord asked Satan again, "Have you noticed my servant, Job? He is the finest man in all the Earth. He is blameless—a man of complete integrity. He fears God and stays away from evil. And he has maintained his integrity, even though you urged me to harm him without cause." Satan replied to the Lord, "Skin for skin! A man will give up everything he has to save his life. But reach out and take away his health, and he will surly curse you to your face!" So, the Lord gave Satan permission again to test Job, but the Lord commanded Satan to spare Job's life. So, Satan left the Lord's presence and struck Job with boils from head to foot.

And yet, Job still had not cursed God. Job scraped his skin with a piece of broken pottery as he sat among the ashes. His wife said to him, "Are you still trying to maintain your integrity? Curse God and die." But Job replied, "You sound like a foolish woman. Should we accept only good things from the hand of God and never anything bad? So, in all this, Job never said anything wrong." You mean to tell me that through all of the chaotic, raging storms and opposition that occurred in Job's life all at once, he still didn't curse God? Job was surely faithful, and because of his faithfulness and God's goodness, the Lord blessed him in the second half of his life even more than in the beginning. For everything he lost, God gave him back double. This was because of his integrity.

What do you do when it looks like living for God (with integrity, might I add) is costing you everything? This includes your relationship, your job, your family, and your friends. When it looks and seems as if you're losing to the world, please trust that you're truly winning in the eyes that matter the most—God's. Regardless of your circumstances, would you be willing to stand firm in your integrity towards the Lord? Always be willing to lay at the Lord's feet what you love. I am not my sin, and you are not your sin. God hates sin, but He loves us! It is truly only God's love, grace and mercy that lures us closer to Him more and more, thus giving us the desire to have a relationship with Him. I am so grateful that I did not have to be perfect to approach God; instead, I was able to go to Him broken and imperfect. It is not your obligation to change before you come to Christ. Our obligation is to surrender our imperfect selves to Him wholeheartedly and allow Christ to do the work in us that needs to be done. It is okay to not have all the answers; it's okay to not have every "t" crossed or every "i" dotted. I will be the first to say that I am imperfect; in-fact, I am thankful that I am flawed because I would not need God if I was a perfect creature. All the same, it is freeing to know that, with God, our identities are secure. God is fighting for you and He's fighting for me! I am speaking beyond the blessings of materialistic possessions. God is fighting for your soul, your love, and your heart of humility.

Heart of Humility

Humility is precious in God's sight. One thing I have come to know through God's Word and through my life's experiences thus far is that God wants our honesty, our hearts, and our humility. God isn't after our money or the materialistic things we tend to grasp, but He is after our hearts. Pride would destroy us faster than humility ever would. When we truly humble ourselves, we can surely confess, "Lord, I am not where I want to be, but I thank you. Lord, I am not where I should be, but I thank you. Lord, I am not where I use to be, so I thank you! Lord, I thank you because I am right where you need me to be." God has promised us in His Word that the work He started in us, He will surely finish. The Bible showed us that a lot of our biblical heroes were not where they wanted to be, but they were exactly where God needed them to be for God to show Himself faithful through them. Proverbs 3:12 says, "The Lord corrects those He love." Therefore, we must allow God to save us from ourselves.

Daily, we are to humble ourselves, examine our hearts, and turn to God in repentance. He cleanses us from all sins, both known and unknown, that could hinder our relationships with Him. Proverbs 15:32-33 states, "If you reject discipline, you only harm yourself; but if you listen to correction, you grow in understanding. Fear of the Lord teaches wisdom; humility precedes honor." As I continue to grow and walk with God, I realize that honor and humility are a package. There is no true honor without humility in Christ, and there's no humility in Christ that God does not honor. Humility serves in the cleansing and pruning process of our hearts, stripping us from pride, ego, and self-sufficiency. The definition of humility, according to Google, is: "a modest or low view of one's own importance; humbleness." The beauty of humility shows up when we allow God to show us ourselves and the sinfulness of our hearts. Just as our physical hearts need oxygen to survive, our spiritual hearts need prayer to survive; this is our spiritual oxygen. In prayer, we relinquish the desire to want to control everything; we relinquish the desire and urge to know it all. However, only in our frailty is logic dismantled in prayer. Prayer is an indication that we do not have all the answers, because we're seeking the one who does—that is God Himself.

Guarding our hearts, above all else, does not entirely prevent us from experiencing offense. In fact, Jesus said in Luke 17:1, "It is impossible but that offenses will come; but woe unto him, through whom they come!" This particular verse lets us know that it's not about avoiding offense as much as it is about us responding to offense in a way that honors God. We do this by choosing to forgive others and by not being bound or entangled by the cords of offense.

I remember working at a plant a few years ago. For the most part, I had some pretty decent co-workers. However, there was one particular co-worker of mine who was very broken and toxic. She was an older woman with identity issues, and those issues had nothing to do with me! She didn't like me because of how others interacted with me. She would try to mimic my hair, my clothes and even my personality! In the beginning, I looked at it as cute! I thought to myself, "Awe, she wants to be like me. How cute!" But cute became weird very fast! The more I sought God about the pseudo identity she presented, the more I realized that her perception of me was far from the identity God had given me. One day, I had a very heated disagreement with her over a stool. Yes, you read that right—a stool, guys! Looking back, I am embarrassed that I allowed myself to get to that level of anger with her. Emotions were high, defenses were up and it was not exactly my best day! Even though she may have been wrong by picking an argument with me, during my prayer time,God told me to apologize to her. My thoughts were loud. "Wait; what?! God did you see everything that just played out?! She doesn't deserve my forgiveness. She's really crazy, Lord, and she's battling internal issues that have absolutely nothing to do with me!" During my devotion and quiet time that morning, God instructed me again to apologize to her. In that moment of prayer, God said, "Erika, you don't deserve my forgiveness, but I give it to you without measure. Do you want my forgiveness?" Mark 11:25 reads, "And when you stand praying, if you hold anything against anyone, forgive them, so that your Father in heaven may forgive you your sins." He went on to say, "Your sin makes you a bit crazy too, but I love you beyond your flaws.

Erika, you have had seeds planted in you that have created identity issues within your heart as well that I am plucking out." Before I knew it, my pride was laid at the feet of Jesus. I responded, "Okay, Lord. I understand, and I will be obedient to what you are leading me to do, but please give me strength!" I went to work that day and God truly granted me the strength I needed to apologize. I no longer saw her from my perspective, but God allowed me to see her the way He sees her, in spite of her brokenness and flaws. I no longer had the self-centered response, "That has nothing to do with me!" Instead, I had genuine empathy in my heart towards her and her flaws. While we were in the women's changing room, I waited patiently until it was just her and I alone in there. My flesh wanted to be petty, but God kindly reminded me that pettiness isn't a fruit of His Spirit; gentleness is. I stopped her before she left out and apologized to her for my behavior and my response to her. Talk about pride on the altar! I even asked her if I could pray with her. (What in the world?! Lord, you said apologize, not pray!) Anyhow, I found myself locking hands and praying with her. Once we finished praying, she apologized to me and said, "Thank you for being mature and apologizing, because I would have never apologized to you." In that moment, I clearly saw that maturity and pettiness have no age. After she left out, I thanked God for the strength He had given me in that moment. He allowed me to see how truly free and lightweight it was to forgive, but to love the unlovable instead. Unforgiveness is truly like drinking poison and expecting the other person to get sick;

it damages your heart and not the other person's. Even after all of that, she was still immature in some of her ways. However, I didn't have to be condescending, petty or immature because God had given me a sense of peace to ignore her nonsense and walk in love towards her; He taught me how to overcome evil with good! I continued to pray for her, all the while enjoying the peace God had given me by forgiving her repeatedly. I am beyond thankful for the way God grew me in that plant. The different kinds of personalities I encountered while working there prepared me for life and ministry in ways I can't fully put into words. God molded my heart and gave me another perspective and a better glimpse of His amazing grace!

Our character is grown and shown in our ability to forgive others from our hearts. This is especially true in a generation that is so determined to cut any and everyone off who doesn't benefit them anymore. Never shut out the opportunity to extend grace and mercy to someone in the same manner that God extends His grace, love and mercy to us daily (see Matthew 18:33). This does not mean that we have to force reconciliation, after all, God often uses people to bless other people! True forgiveness is being able to bless people, not just in the physical realm but the spiritual realm as well. Even those who may have hurt, offended, or persecuted you in some way, shape, or form! If we are only able to love people when they are the most lovable or beneficial to us, it goes without saying that we're in error! One thing I've come to notice is that God frequently tests our hearts and our character. What's in your heart will show up in your character. How do you treat people you think you may not need? How do you show grace and mercy in your life? What do you do when no one is looking, when no one is clapping, when no one is laughing with you, or riding with you? This is why it is important to always examine our motives. Psalm 139:23 says, "Search me, God, and know my heart; test me and know my anxious thoughts. See if there is any offensive way in me; and lead me in the way everlasting." Proverbs 16:2 states, "All a person's ways seem pure to them, but motives are weighed by the Lord." Always strive to become a person of integrity, whether in public or private.

Portions

What we consume and what we do not consume all play a very important role in our spiritual health as well as our physical health. Full disclaimer!!! I am by no means a medical doctor. I am just a living vessel for the Kingdom of God who enjoys passing along the information God has given me to share. Let us continue.

When we think about the word "portion", we often think about how much of something we may or may not have, and how much of something we are allowed to consume. Overeating or eating too much salt can lead to high blood pressure, heart disease, and health problems. If what we consume physically, whether good or bad, can affect the well-being of our hearts, then surely what we consume spiritually, whether good or bad, can intrude on the well-being of our hearts as well.

I can recall= spending time in God's presence on a Tuesday afternoon, journaling to Him whatever my heart poured out. All of a sudden, the spirit of anxiety tried to overwhelm me. As I laid on my living room floor soaked in my tears, I was reminded of Philippians 4:6-7, which reads, "Be anxious for nothing, but in everything by prayer and supplication with thanksgiving let your requests be made known to God. And the peace of God which surpasses all understanding will guard your hearts and minds through Jesus Christ." As I was reminded of that truth, the Lord gave me such a simple, yet profound, revelation. I sat there, wiped the tears from my eyes, and looked around. When I'd first moved into my apartment, my living room was empty! Even though I desired to have a fully furnished living room and much more, I didn't have anything but my dining room table. I had gotten rid of my old furniture before moving into my new place because I wanted to make space for something new. Now, I know you are wondering and perhaps asking the question, "Erika, what in the world does all of this have to do with portions?" Bear with me; I am going somewhere with this.

Even though I did not have the funds at that moment to get what I wanted, what I did have was hope and faith that I would eventually be able to purchase new furniture. Over time, my living room began to become a lot cozier. I first purchased my dining room table, and then I purchased my couch. After this, I purchased a rug, followed by a book stand, my décor, and lastly, my desk. God revealed to me that He did not provide me with everything I may have wanted or thought I needed in that moment. My living room came together in portions. As I sat there relating the same scenario to my life, it gave me a sense of peace, and I hope that the illustration and understanding provides peace to you as well. You may not be where you want to be or have what you desire to have, but God is blessing us a portion at a time in accordance with His will and not our own timelines. We must guard our hearts wisely from the seed and fruit of discontentment.

Discontentment is very detrimental to our hearts, both physically and spiritually. If we are not consciously guarding our hearts from the scrutiny of discontentment, we will be easily enticed by our own lack of gratitude. Gratitude shifts our perspectives to what is important. It teaches our hearts to identify what matters the most. It challenges the innermost parts of us because we are spiritual beings. Pure gratitude weighs the desires of our hearts on a Godly scale. It is easy to get caught up in what you do not have or what you are striving to get, but in the midst of doing this, our gratitude for what we have is overshadowed by what we do not have. This leads us to become anxious, weary, drained, depressed, and ungrateful. Simply put, it causes us to chase the wind. We all desire more, and God places some of those desires in our hearts, however, finding contentment in what He has already provided for and to us is great gain! You now have what you once prayed for. We must not bypass the opportunity to always be thankful for those answered prayers. The Bible tells us, in Proverbs 13:12-14, "Hope deferred makes the heart sick, but a desire fulfilled is a tree of life." Google defines hope as: "a feeling of expectation and desire for a certain thing to happen." Biblical hope is faith, not a feeling. "Faith is the substance of things hoped for and the evidence of things not seen." When that expectation and yearning is deferred (delayed), it can cause the heart to become debilitated.

Finding contentment in every circumstance is pleasing to God, regardless of whether you are waiting and hoping for marriage, a better career, the salvation of a loved one, to become a parent, to make new friends, or to fulfill your purpose in life, please note that contentment DOES NOT await you in the fulfillment of that desire! Be grateful; there is always joy in gratitude. No one is exempt from discontentment. We all have a choice to make. Unfortunately, trouble is inevitable. We are all presented with free-will; we can allow ourselves to be tormented by what we see or feel; we can let Satan bind us with the cords of anxiety, anger, or fear. Then again, we can make the conscious decision to allow God to bless us with an inner peace that only He can give. This allows our perspectives to shift and our countenances to reflect that shift.

Watering the seed of contentment within our hearts produces the assurance and security of God's sovereignty. God knows where we are now, and only He knows where we will be later. With that in mind, I have now come to an understanding that I do not have to rush ahead of God to finish the work He has started in me, and neither do you! Be still and know that He is God all by Himself (see Psalms 46:10). A while back, this particular scripture was one of my favorite go-to verses because it allowed me to justify disobeying God by procrastinating to do what He'd told me to do, or so I assumed. One evening, I was a bit overwhelmed and I did not want to do what I should have been doing in that moment, so I allowed an excuse to form in my mind, along with the aforementioned scripture, but the Holy Spirit would not allow me to be great in my complacency. Ha! Instead, I was led to break down the verse so that I could understand it and use the verse in its proper context. "Be still and know that I am God" does not necessarily mean to stop working and procrastinate.

The definition for working, according to Google, means: "functioning or able to function/ the action of doing the work." Google defines the word waiting as: "the action of staying where one is or delaying action until a particular time or until something else happens." In essence, the difference between working and waiting indicates that we are to diligently work on what God has instructed us to do as He intervenes and does what we are unable to do. When we are able to acknowledge the unfruitful negative seeds that were planted in our hearts, whether through others or of our own doing, God can only then uproot those toxic or barren seeds.

Now that I am a wife and mother of twin baby girls, the posture of my heart is more crucial than ever before. The health of my heart will affect them, both knowingly and unknowingly. I cannot afford to stop guarding my heart, and neither can you! Above all else, guard your heart for out of it flows the issues of life!

Heavenly Father, let the meditation of our hearts and the words of our mouths be acceptable in your sight. Thank you for extending your grace to us in the moments when we have fallen short of your glory. Remind us of the blessing of closed doors, even when we see those shut doors as the evidence of our failure or as missed opportunities. Strengthen us so that we can continue to grow in the grace and knowledge of Jesus Christ. May our identities be grounded in your truth, after all, you told us that if anyone is in Christ, that individual is a new creation—the old has passed away and all things have become new because of your unmerited favor. Help us to be mindful of your presence everyday, and may your grace forever abound. Amen.

www.ingramcontent.com/pod-product-compliance
Lightning Source LLC
LaVergne TN
LVHW052036080426
835513LV00018B/2353